JumpStart Your Thinking

Books by Dr. John C. Maxwell
Can Teach You How to Be a REAL Success

Relationships

25 Ways to Win with People
Becoming a Person of Influence
Encouragement Changes Everything
Ethics 101
*Everyone Communicates,
Few Connect*
The Power of Partnership
Relationships 101
Winning With People

Equipping

The 15 Invaluable Laws of Growth
*The 17 Essential Qualities
of a Team Player*
*The 17 Indisputable Laws
of Teamwork*
Developing the Leaders Around You
Equipping 101
Intentional Living
JumpStart Your Growth
Learning from the Giants
Make Today Count
Mentoring 101
My Dream Map
Partners in Prayer
Put Your Dream to the Test
Running with the Giants
Talent Is Never Enough
Today Matters
Wisdom from Women in the Bible
Your Road Map for Success

Attitude

Attitude 101
The Difference Maker
Failing Forward
How Successful People Think
How Successful People Win
*Sometimes You Win,
Sometimes You Learn*
Success 101
Thinking for a Change
The Winning Attitude

Leadership

*The 10th Anniversary Edition
of The 21 Irrefutable Laws
of Leadership*
*The 21 Indispensable Qualities
of a Leader*
*The 21 Most Powerful Minutes
in a Leader's Day*
The 360 Degree Leader
Developing the Leader Within You
The 5 Levels of Leadership
Go for Gold
JumpStart Your Leadership
Leadership 101
Leadership Gold
*Leadership Promises for
Every Day*

A 90-DAY
IMPROVEMENT
PLAN

JumpStart Your Thinking

JOHN C. MAXWELL

CENTER
STREET

NEW YORK BOSTON NASHVILLE

The author is represented by Yates & Yates, LLP, Literary Agency, Orange, California.

Literary development and design: Koechel Peterson & Associates, Inc., Minneapolis, Minnesota.

This book has been adapted from *Thinking for a Change*, copyright © 2003 by John C. Maxwell. Published by Center Street.

Center Street
Hachette Book Group
1290 Avenue of the Americas
New York, NY 10104

www.CenterStreet.com

Printed in the United States of America

RRD-C

First trade edition: December 2015
10 9 8 7 6 5 4 3 2 1

Center Street is a division of Hachette Book Group, Inc.
The Center Street name and logo are trademarks of Hachette Book Group, Inc.

The Hachette Speakers Bureau provides a wide range of authors for speaking events. To find out more, go to www.hachettespeakersbureau.com or call (866) 376-6591.

The publisher is not responsible for websites (or their content) that are not owned by the publisher.

ISBN 978-1-4555-8834-3

INTRODUCTION

*P*erhaps you've wondered, as I often have, why it is that some people are successful and others are not. I've looked for answers to that question throughout my life. In the process, I've also asked myself if there is one thing that all successful people have in common. What one thing separates those who go to the top from those who never seem to get there?

The answer is not that some people get better opportunities and better educations or that some people are just lazy and had bad breaks. The answer is: *Good Thinking!* Those who embrace good thinking as a lifestyle understand the relationship between their level of thinking and their level of progress. They also realize that to change their lives, they must change their thinking.

Here's the simple difference: *Successful people think differently than unsuccessful people.*

That's why I'm excited that you want to jumpstart your thinking. I've been a student of good thinking all my life, so I know how important it is for making progress. It's something I first learned from my father, Melvin Maxwell, because he is an example of someone who changed his life as a result of changing his thinking.

If you met my dad, he would tell you that he was born with a naturally negative bent to his thinking. In addition, he grew up during the Depression, and when he was six years old, his mother died. He was not a happy or hopeful child. But as a teenager, he began to see that all the successful people he knew had one thing in common: They filled their lives with positive thoughts about themselves and others. He desired to be successful like them, so he embarked on the daily task of changing his thinking. To his delight, after much time and effort, his thinking changed him.

People who know him today see Dad as a totally positive person. They would be surprised to find out that he started his life with a negative mind-set. This change in his thinking allowed him to rise to a level of living that seemed above his potential. He went on to be the most successful person in his professional circle. He became a college president and touched the lives of innumerable people. To this day he is my hero.

So how skilled is your thinking? Does your thinking help you achieve? If you're currently not successful, or you're not as successful as you would like to be, it may be because you need to jumpstart your thinking.

I am very excited to present you with this 90-day plan to improve your thinking, because to do well in life, we must first think well. The way you think really impacts every aspect of your life. It doesn't matter whether you are an entreprenuer, teacher, parent, scientist, or corporate executive. Good thinking will improve your life. It will help you to become an achiever.

Over the next 90 days, you will be provided with ideas and action steps to help you make the best use of your most precious possession: your mind. You'll discover that new mental habits can be learned and that by changing them, you can change your life. Drawing from some of the best thinkers in history, you will learn specific techniques on *how* to think, not what to think. You will see an immediate impact and open the door to new possibilities.

What will it take for you to jumpstart your thinking? Consistently set aside 15 minutes every day for the next 90 days to think intentionally about how you think. Read and consider the inspirational quote for the day, read and digest the lesson, and move forward by taking action in response to the question.

If you spend time implementing the kind of successful thinking described in the daily readings for the next three months, you will place yourself on the pathway of success. It could be the difference that makes all the difference in your life!

Ready? Let's get started!

DAY

1

You are today where your thoughts have brought you.
You will be tomorrow where your thoughts take you.
JAMES ALLEN

Changing from negative to positive thinking will transform a person's life, but it isn't always easy, especially if you have a difficult time with change. For some, it's a lifelong struggle. Do you know what most people's number one challenge is when it comes to making positive personal changes? It's their feelings. They want to change, but they don't know how to get past their emotions. But there is a way to do it. Consider the truth contained in the following syllogism:

Major Premise: I can control my thoughts.

Minor Premise: My feelings come from my thoughts.

Conclusion: I can control my feelings by controlling my thoughts.

If you are willing to change your thinking, you can change your feelings. If you change your feelings, you can change your actions. And changing your actions—based on good thinking—can change your life. That truth has the power to set you free.

Make a list of words that describe your thoughts and feelings. Circle the negative ones, and make a decision to start improving them.

DAY

2

*Thought is the original source of all wealth,
all success, all material gain, all great discoveries
and inventions, and all achievement.*
CLAUDE M. BRISTOL

It may seem obvious that the quality of people's thinking leads to the quality of their results. However, one of the reasons people don't achieve their dreams is that they desire to change their results without changing their thinking. That's never going to work. If you want to jumpstart your thinking, you must believe that only good thinking creates the foundation for good results.

In *As a Man Thinketh*, James Allen, philosopher of the human spirit, wrote, "Good thoughts and actions can never produce bad results; bad thoughts and actions can never produce good results. This is but saying that nothing can come from corn but corn, nothing from nettles but nettles." Simply put, if you expect to reap corn when you plant nettles, you're not going to get corn—no matter how much time you spend watering, fertilizing, or cultivating your plants. If you don't like the crop you are reaping, you need to change the seed you are sowing!

Do you want to achieve? Then sow the "seed" of good thinking.

Where in life are you failing to get the results you want? What aspect of your thinking might be leading to those results? What changes in your thinking might be required to produce the good results you desire?

DAY

3

Beware when the great God
lets loose a great thinker on the planet.
RALPH WALDO EMERSON

Do you realize that the quality of your thinking is the lid for your potential? To paraphrase the words of King Solomon, wisest of all ancient kings, "As people think in their hearts, so they are." If you're an excellent thinker, you have excellent potential; but if your thinking is poor, you have a lid on your life.

Sam Walton, the founder of Wal-Mart, refused to believe the popular notion that a town of less than 50,000 in population could not support a discount store for very long. He thought for himself and struck out on his own. Today Wal-Mart is the world's largest retailer and company by revenue, employing more than two million people. How's that for potential! No wonder Jack Welch, former chairman of General Electric, said, "The hero is the one with ideas."

The greatest detriment to your potential success tomorrow is your thinking today. If your thinking is limited, so is your potential. But if you can keep growing in your thinking, you will constantly outgrow what you're doing. And your potential will always be off the charts!

Name the best thinkers you know personally. Describe what's different about them. Choose one of those thinkers and try to arrange to spend some time with him or her.

DAY

*An invasion of armies can be resisted,
but not an invasion of ideas.*
Victor Hugo

Here's some good news as you begin your thinking journey: No matter how complicated life gets or how difficult problems may seem, good thinking can make a difference—*if* you make it a consistent part of your life. The more you engage in good thinking, the more good thoughts will come to you. Success comes to those who habitually do things that unsuccessful people don't do. Achievement comes from the habit of good thinking. The more you engage in good thinking, the more good thoughts you will continue to think. It's like creating a never-ending army of ideas capable of achieving almost anything.

If you're like many people, you believe good thinking is so complicated that it lies beyond your reach. But in truth, it's really a very simple process. Every person has the potential to become a better thinker. I've observed that unsuccessful people focus their thinking on survival, average people focus on maintenance, and successful people focus on progress. A change of thinking can help you move from survival or maintenance to real progress. Ninety-five percent of achieving anything is knowing what you want and paying the price to get it.

Where do you focus your thinking—on survival, on maintenance, or on progress? What change of thinking can help you move from survival or maintenance to real progress?

DAY

5

Nothing limits achievement like small thinking; nothing expands possibilities like unleashed thinking.
WILLIAM ARTHUR WARD

Did you know that good thinking isn't just one thing? It consists of several specific thinking skills. Becoming a good thinker means developing all the thinking "pieces" to become the kind of person who can achieve great things. Throughout the rest of this book, we'll focus on the following types of thinking:

- *Big-picture Thinking*
- *Focused Thinking*
- *Creative Thinking*
- *Realistic Thinking*
- *Strategic Thinking*
- *Possibility Thinking*
- *Reflective Thinking*
- *Uncommon Thinking*
- *Shared Thinking*
- *Unselfish Thinking*
- *Bottom-line Thinking*

These are your building blocks. If you develop each of these kinds of thinking, you will become a better thinker and your life will change.

In the past, how have you defined good thinking? Considering these building blocks, how would you describe it now?

DAY

6

*Nurture great thoughts, for you
will never go higher than your thoughts.*
BENJAMIN DISRAELI

What difference can a shift in your thinking make? Jack Welch, former CEO of General Electric, gave this advice to a young businessperson who asked him how he could elevate himself among all of his other associates:

"The only way to get out of the pile and stand out to your boss is to understand this simple principle: When he asks you a question, assigns a basic project, or sends you out to gather some data, he simply wants you to go out and confirm what he already believes is true. If you want to elevate yourself, you must sink your thoughts and time into not only answering the question, but three or more other ideas, options, and perspectives that were probably not previously considered by your boss. The goal is to add value to the idea and the thought by exceeding expectations when the question is given to you. Because 99.9 percent of all employees are in the pile because they don't think, you will always be given more critical questions to answer. And in time, you will be the one giving out the questions to others!"

If you desire to climb up out of the pile, become the best thinker you can be.

Describe your desire for success and to improve your life. Write a declaration of commitment to change your thinking. Then sign and date it.

....
....
....
....
....
....
....
....

....
....
....
....
....
....
....
....
....
....
....
....

DAY

7

People will never attain what they cannot see themselves doing.
KAREN FORD

Over the next six days, I want you to see how you can begin to change yourself as you take responsibility to change your thinking. If you follow the process faithfully, it will result in a changed life!

Step 1: *Changing your thinking changes your beliefs.* My friend author Gordon MacDonald says that if you do not believe in yourself, you will "fall victim to ideas and systems that are destructive to the human spirit and to human relationships . . . and grow dependent upon the thoughts and opinions of others." Or you may simply give up.

But here's the good news: Even if you currently lack what MacDonald calls "a strong mind," there's no reason to give up or live an unfulfilling life. The human mind *can* change, *if* you are willing to put in the effort to change your thinking. As you strive to change your thinking, tell yourself these three things:

Change is Personal—I *need* to change.

Change is Possible—I'm *able* to change.

Change is Profitable—I'll be *rewarded* by change.

Remember, no matter how old you are or what your circumstances may be, you can change your thinking. And when you change your thinking, you change your beliefs.

Describe a personal or professional issue that has created an ongoing obstacle to your progress. What change in your thinking do you need to make to change what you believe about this obstacle?

DAY

8

*The first and most important step toward success
is the expectation that we can succeed.*

NELSON BOSWELL

Yesterday I stated that when you change your thinking, you change your beliefs. When your belief in your personal abilities changes, it will transform you. Why is that a foundational fact? Because a belief is not just an idea that you possess; it is an idea that possesses you. A belief holds great power, because it changes an individual's expectations, which bring us to Step 2: *Changing your beliefs changes your expectations.*

When you begin to change your thinking and build your beliefs on a new foundation of personal growth, you have more than just hope and a dream to carry you forward. You will expect to achieve your goal because you determined to change yourself and you've done the hard work of changing to prepare for it. You're ready. You will expect to succeed, and you will.

The words of billionaire entrepreneur Richard M. DeVos are true: "The only thing that stands between a man and what he wants from life is often merely the will to try it and the faith to believe that it is possible."

Continuing with yesterday's action, how does changing your beliefs about the ongoing obstacle to your progress change your expectations regarding it? Describe the change.

DAY

9

*There is no medicine like hope,
no incentive so great, and no tonic so powerful
as expectation of something tomorrow.*
ORISON S. MARDEN

A dejected young man had just had his palm read by a carnival fortune teller who told him that he would be poor and unhappy until he was forty-five. Then he had a thought. "What will happen when I'm forty-five?" She replied, "You'll get used to it."

Our expectations have a tremendous impact on our attitudes. Ben Franklin quipped, "Blessed is he who expects nothing, for he shall receive it." Negative expectations are a quick route to dead-end thinking.

The good news is that when you change your thinking, you change your beliefs, which change your expectations, and *changing your expectations changes your attitude*. That is Step 3 to changing yourself.

How many successful people do you know who are apathetic or negative? Positive expectations bring a positive attitude. They produce excitement, conviction, desire, confidence, commitment, and energy—all characteristics that help a person to achieve success. If you would like to possess these qualities in greater abundance, raise your expectations.

Continuing with yesterday's action, how does changing your expectations about the ongoing obstacle to your progress change your attitude regarding it?

DAY

10

Our emotions are the driving powers of our lives.
EARL RINEY

Have you ever observed how your mood affects the way you act? When you feel particularly happy, are you more energized and more likely to be kind to others, and do you take on tasks more readily and complete them with confidence and competence? How about when you're having a really bad day? Do you get less work done and are less patient with your family and colleagues?

An attitude is little more than a mood or predominant emotion sustained over time. It is the "advance man" of our true selves. Its roots are inward but its fruit is outward. It is our best friend or our worst enemy. It is more honest and more consistent than our words. It is an outward look based on past experiences. It is a thing that draws people to us or repels them. It is never content until it is expressed. It is the librarian of our past, the speaker of our present, and the prophet of our future.

Psychologist William James said, "That which holds our attention determines our action." In other words, your behavior follows your attitude. The two cannot be separated. This brings us to the importance of Step 4 in changing yourself: *Changing your attitude changes your behavior,* and that changes everything.

Continuing with yesterday's action, how does changing your attitude about the ongoing obstacle to your progress change your behavior regarding it?

DAY

11

We do not suddenly become what we do not cooperate in becoming.
WILLIAM J. BENNETT

In my twenties, I enjoyed the game of golf, but my performance left a lot to be desired. A golf professional advised me that I would never improve unless I changed my grip. He showed me the proper way to hold the club, which felt terrible to me. When I complained that I didn't know if I'd ever be able to do it that way, he answered, "Then you'll never get any better." My performance depended on a change in behavior that first required a change in my attitude.

The steps I went through to change my golf game are the same steps required in changing ourselves. Changing your thinking changes your beliefs; changing your beliefs changes your expectations; changing your expectations changes your attitude; changing your attitude changes your behavior, and Step 5: *Changing your behavior changes your performance.*

Don't ever be too impressed with goal setting; be impressed with goal *getting.* Reaching new goals and moving to a higher level of performance—that is, what you do on a constant basis—always requires change, and change feels awkward. But take comfort in the knowledge that if a change doesn't feel uncomfortable, it's probably not really a change.

Continuing with yesterday's action, how does changing your behavior about the ongoing obstacle to your progress change your performance regarding it?

DAY

12

*It is the man who carefully advances step by step,
with his mind becoming wider and wider—and
progressively better able to grasp any theme or situation . . .
who is bound to succeed in the greatest degree.*

Alexander Graham Bell

When you change your performance, you have the power to reach Step 6. *Changing your performance changes your life.* Here's how it has worked out in my life:

Four and a half decades ago, let's just say I was less than an inspiring speaker. To change my performance, I knew that I could not approach communication in the same way mentally and still perform differently. I began by studying respected speakers—how they connected with their audiences—and I copied them. It took me eight challenging years to learn how to be myself before an audience and to develop my own style. Becoming a better communicator required a whole new way of thinking, and it felt uncomfortable. But I did it, and each year I speak in person to more than 350,000 people.

I'm still a student of communication. I know that if I keep improving my thinking, it will impact my beliefs, which change my expectations, which affect my attitude, which changes my behavior, which improves my performance. And that will change my life.

Continuing with yesterday's action, how does changing your performance about the ongoing obstacle to your progress change your life?

DAY

13

For the flower to blossom, you need the right soil as well as the right seed. The same is true to cultivate good thinking.
WILLIAM BERNBACH

Becoming a good thinker isn't overly complicated. It's a discipline, and like most disciplines, it can be cultivated and refined. That's why over the next eight days I want to teach you the process that I've used to discover and develop good thoughts. It's certainly not the only one that works, but it has worked well for me.

First, you need to *find a place to think your thoughts*. Where is the best place to think? Everybody's different. For some people it's in the shower or going to a park. For me, the best places to think are in the thinking chair in my home office and in the pool while I'm swimming laps. I keep my iPad or a pen and paper on my nightstand for ideas that come to me when I'm in bed.

I believe I often get thoughts because I make it a habit to frequently go to my thinking places. If you want to consistently generate ideas, you need to do the same thing. Find a place where you can think, and plan to capture your thoughts on paper so that you don't lose them. When I found a place to think my thoughts, my thoughts found a place in me.

If you don't already have a good thinking place, you need to find one. Where will you choose to create your thoughts?

DAY

14

Learning to write is learning to think. You don't know anything clearly unless you can state it in writing.

S. I. HAYAKAWA

To become a good thinker, the second thing you need to do is to *find a place to shape your thoughts*. This may or may not be the same place as your thinking place. Rarely do ideas come fully formed and completely worked out. Most of the time, they need to be shaped until they have substance. As my friend Dan Reiland says, they have to "stand the test of clarity and questioning." During the shaping time, you want to hold an idea up to strong scrutiny. Many times a thought that seemed outstanding late at night looks pretty silly in the light of day.

You can shape your thoughts almost anywhere. Just find a place that works for you, where you will be able to write things down, focus your attention without interruptions, and ask questions about your ideas. By asking questions, you gain perspective on your ideas. Fine tune them. One of the best ways to do that is to put your thoughts in writing. As you shape your thoughts, you find out whether an idea has potential. You also learn some things about yourself. As I have tried to shape my thoughts, I have often realized that my thoughts have shaped me.

Describe one of the current ideas that you've been thinking about and begin to shape it here. Put your thoughts, including your questions about your idea, in writing and fine tune them.

DAY

*Thought is, perhaps, the forerunner and
even the mother of ideas, and ideas are the most
powerful and the most useful things in the world.*
GEORGE GARDNER

If you come upon great thoughts and spend time
mentally shaping them, don't stop there. If you do, you'll
miss some of the most valuable aspects of the thinking
process. If you really want to take an idea to the highest
level, *find people to stretch your thoughts*—ask others to
help you expand your ideas to their greatest potential.

I've found a formula that can help. It says, the Right
Thought plus the Right *People* in the Right *Environment*
at the Right *Time* for the Right *Reason* = the *Right Result*.
This combination is hard to beat. Here's why:

When you expose the seed of the right idea to the
right people, that original thought often grows, along with
its vision, power, and impact. Who are the right people to
stretch a vision? They are ones who love you and embrace
your vision, who know you and strengthen your vision,
and who complement you and enlarge your vision. They
are the few who stretch a thought before you land it with
many. Make it a goal to find people who will stretch you
to your potential and add value to you in areas that are
important to you.

Who are the good thinking partners in your life? List them here, and describe how they stretch your thoughts. If you don't have any, begin seeking out some.

DAY

16

To be right too soon is to be wrong.
EMPEROR HADRIAN

Once you find the right people to help stretch your thoughts, *find the right environment to expand them.* In the right environment thinking is valued, ideas flow freely, fresh eyes are welcome, change is expected, questions are encouraged, egos are checked, ideas stimulate better ideas, and thinking generates teamwork. If you're stuck in a wrong environment, find one that encourages you.

Ideas are fragile things when they first see the light of day. If you try to implement them too early or introduce them while there are more naysayers than supporters, they won't survive. While still in the stretching stage of an idea, present it without time frames or rigidly defined goals. Let the idea breathe before you harness it.

Every thought has the potential to become something great. When you find a place to stretch your thoughts, you find that potential and it gives you a chance to take that idea as far as it can go. Sometimes a thought is merely a springboard to a greater idea. As I have tried to stretch my thinking, I have discovered that my thinking has stretched me.

If you've begun to make progress on the issue that you began to shape your thoughts around two days ago, get together the good thinkers in your life to help you stretch it. Or meet with them to talk about another challenge you face. Write your fine-tuned thoughts here and your objectives from the meeting.

DAY

17

Great ideas need landing gear as well as wings.
C. D. JACKSON

Any idea that remains only an idea doesn't make an impact. The real power of an idea comes when you *find a place to land your thoughts* with others so that they can be implemented. As you plan for the application phase of the thinking process, land your ideas first with yourself. People will buy into an idea only after they buy into the leader who communicates it. If you are unsure about it, it won't fly.

Next, you must help influencers to embrace it. After all, they are the people who carry thoughts from idea to implementation. Landing an idea with the influencers in your organization will increase your influence. Then once you've done that, move your idea to those most affected by it. Landing thoughts with the people closest to changes that occur as a result of a new idea can give you a "reality read." And that's important, because sometimes even when you've diligently completed the process of creating a thought, shaping it, and stretching it with other good thinkers, you can still miss the mark.

Consider an idea that you want to "land" by enlisting other people to work with you on implementing it. Once you've landed it with yourself, identify the influencers who will need to embrace it for it to succeed. Plan how you will connect with them.

DAY

Think like a man of action—act like a man of thought.
HENRI-LOUIS BERGSON

What good is thinking if it has no application in real life? Thinking divorced from actions cannot be productive. Learning how to master the process of thinking well leads you to productive thinking. If you can develop the discipline of good thinking and turn it into a lifetime habit, you will be productive all of your life. Once you've created, shaped, stretched, and landed your thoughts, you need to *find a place to fly your thoughts*.

I've observed that high achievers have a natural tendency to jump into any project and start working; they are usually people of action who possess high energy. But to get the kind of results you want—to fly your thoughts well—give your plans the right amount of thinking time, and you'll find that the implementation time decreases and the results get better. Your thinking time is like the runway of an airport. Just as larger planes need a longer runway to fly, big ideas need a long runway of thinking to get launched. As I have tried to fly my thoughts, I have found that my thoughts have taken me to new heights.

Consider an idea that is important to you. Detail your thoughts on how you will implement the idea for maximum results.

DAY

I am still learning.
MICHELANGELO

Do you want to master the process of good thinking? Then I recommend that you *expose yourself to good input and good thinkers.* Good thinkers always prime the pump of ideas. They always look for things to get the thinking process started. Read books, review trade magazines, listen to audiobooks and podcasts, engage in programs, watch videos, and spend time with good thinkers. And when something intrigues you—whether it's someone else's idea or the seed of an idea that you've come up with yourself—put it in writing and keep it somewhere in your favorite thinking place to stimulate your thinking. My favorite place to keep ideas that need reflection is a half-sheet sized portfolio that I keep with me. It's my thinking companion.

Next, I recommend that you *choose to think good thoughts.* You must become intentional about the thinking process. Regularly put yourself in the right place to think, shape, stretch, and land your thoughts. Make it a priority. Set up a "thinking schedule" and method of your own. No matter what you choose to do, go to your thinking place, take paper and pen, and make sure you capture your ideas in writing. Remember, thinking is a discipline.

To what good input—magazines, books, audio programs, or videos—are you regularly exposing yourself to and challenging yourself as a thinker? List them.

DAY

20

*I can give you a six-word formula for success:
Think things through—then follow through.*

EDDIE RICKENBACKER

To master the process of good thinking, I also recommend that you *act on your good thoughts*, because many ideas have a short shelf life. You must follow through on them before the expiration date.

For some people, the greatest challenge to becoming a good thinker is the past hurts or current worries that prevent them from spending productive time thinking. To start the thinking process, you cannot wait until you feel like thinking to do it. However, I've found that once you engage in the process of good thinking, you can *use your emotions to feed the process and create mental momentum*. After you go through the disciplined process of thinking and enjoy some success, savor the moment and try riding the mental energy of that success. It's likely to spur additional productive ideas.

Finally, *repeat the process*. One good thought does not make a good life. The people who have one good thought and try to ride it for an entire career often end up unhappy or destitute. Success comes to those who have an entire mountain of gold that they continually mine, not those who find one nugget and try to live on it.

What steps will you take today to cultivate the habit of giving birth to, nurturing, and developing great thoughts every day? Schedule those steps and follow through.

DAY

21

Where success is concerned, people are not measured in inches, or pounds, or college degrees, or family background; they are measured by the size of their thinking.

DAVID J. SCHWARTZ

If you want to be successful, one thinking skill you need is to *acquire the wisdom of big-picture thinking*. Real estate developer Donald Trump quipped, "You have to think anyway, so why not think big?" Big-picture thinking brings wholeness and maturity to a person's thinking. It brings perspective. It's like making the frame of a picture larger, in the process expanding not only what you can see but also what you are able to do.

Big-picture thinkers are never satisfied with what they already know. They are lifelong learners—always visiting new places, reading new books, meeting new people, learning new skills. And because of that practice, they often are able to connect the unconnected.

To help me maintain a learner's attitude, I spend a few moments every morning reviewing my calendar and to-do list and noting where I am most likely to learn something. Then I mentally cue myself to look attentively for something that will improve me in that situation. If you desire to keep learning, examine every day and look for opportunities to learn.

On a scale of 1 to 10, with 1 being narrow and 10 being expansive, how do you rate as a big-picture thinker? Do you see the whole picture, or are you more likely to focus on just one aspect? What will you work at today to become a better big-picture thinker?

DAY

22

Many an object is not seen, though it falls within the range of our visual ray, because it does not come within the range of our intellectual ray.

HENRY DAVID THOREAU

Big-picture thinkers search for opportunities to broaden their experience by *listening intentionally* to others who have expertise in areas where they don't. When you find opportunities to meet with such people, bring an agenda and ask penetrating questions to enlarge your understanding and to know how to apply the answers to your life.

Big-picture thinkers also realize that other people bring a valuable perspective to situations that are different than their own, and they make an effort to see other people's worlds through their eyes. To *see how others see*, you must first find out how they think. Becoming a good listener helps with that. So does getting over your personal agenda and trying to take the other person's perspective.

Becoming a big-picture thinker can help you to *live with wholeness.* You expand your experience because you expand your world. As a result, you will accomplish more than narrow-minded people. And you will experience fewer unwanted surprises, too, because you are more likely to see the many components involved in any given situation: issues, people, relationships, timing, and values.

On a scale of 1 to 10, with 1 being poor and 10 being excellent, how do you rate as a listener? Take an opportunity today to listen intentionally to someone on your team or in your family without interrupting. Write down what you learned by listening carefully.

DAY

23

Big thinking precedes great achievement.
WILFRED PETERSON

Intuitively, you probably recognize big-picture thinking as beneficial. Few people want to be closed-minded. But just in case you're not completely convinced, consider these reasons why you should make the effort to become a better big-picture thinker:

Big-picture thinking allows you to lead—to see and communicate the vision, size up situations, show how the future connects with the past, and seize opportune moments.

Big-picture thinking keeps you on target to get the right things done.

Big-picture thinking allows you to see what others see.

Big-picture thinking promotes teamwork. The better the grasp team members have of the big picture, the greater their potential to work together as a team.

Big-picture thinking keeps you from being caught up in the mundane, because you don't lose sight of the all-important overview.

Big-picture thinking helps you to chart uncharted territory—you must be able to look beyond the immediate and see the big picture.

In what specific ways will you benefit the most from becoming a big-picture thinker? In what areas of your thinking do you need to work the hardest to expand your thinking?

DAY

24

In order to properly understand the big picture, everyone should fear becoming mentally clouded and obsessed with one small section of truth.

XUN ZI

If you desire to seize new opportunities and open new horizons, you need to add big-picture thinking to your abilities. To become better able to see the big picture, *don't strive for certainty*. Big-picture thinkers are comfortable with ambiguity. They don't try to force every observation or piece of data into preformulated mental cubbyholes. They think broadly and can juggle many seemingly contradictory thoughts in their minds.

In *The Five Temptations of a CEO*, management consultant Patrick Lencioni warned that CEOs should not try to pursue harmony. Instead, they should embrace healthy, productive conflict. Nor should they aim for certainty. Instead, they should try to find clarity. To cultivate the ability to think big picture, you must get in the habit of bringing together complex and diverse concepts, accepting seemingly opposite points of view at the same time, and embracing what authors James Collins and Jerry Porras call the "Genius of the AND" in their book *Built to Last*. In business, for example, pursue purpose AND profit, embrace core values AND innovation, be highly visionary AND execute the details well.

Think of a past problem or current project that you would like to improve through big-picture thinking. Write what you see as the obvious solution for success, then write an alternate solution that seems to contradict the first idea. How can you make these seemingly contradictory ideas work together?

DAY

25

People fail forward to success.
MARY KAY ASH

To become a good thinker better able to see the big picture, *learn from every experience.* Big-picture thinkers broaden their outlook by striving to learn from every experience. They don't rest on their successes; they learn from them. More importantly, they learn from their failures. They can do that because they remain teachable.

In my book *Failing Forward*, I described a teachable spirit as "an attitude, a mind-set that says, 'No matter how much I know (or think I know), I can learn from this situation.' That kind of thinking can help you turn adversity into advantage. It can make you a winner even during the most difficult circumstances."

Varied experiences—both positive and negative— help you see the big picture. The greater the variety of experience and success, the more potential to learn you have. If you desire to be a big-picture thinker, get out there and try a lot of things, take a lot of chances, and take time to learn after every victory or defeat.

At the end of today, review what you learned on this day—both positive and negative. Capture those thoughts in writing and file them so that you can retrieve and use them in the future. Make this a regular part of your daily routine.

DAY

26

To know the road ahead, ask those coming back.
CHINESE PROVERB

Big-picture thinkers learn from their experiences, but also from experiences they don't have. That is, they *gain insight from a variety of people*—from customers, employees, colleagues, and leaders. My friend Kevin Myers meets with a group of younger men to mentor them and answer their questions and share his experiences. Every once in a while, Kevin also meets me for lunch, armed with questions he wants to ask me. Does he do it because I'm more intelligent or talented than he is? No. I just have fifteen years more experience than he does, and he benefits from the lessons I've learned.

If you desire to broaden your thinking and see more of the big picture, seek out counselors to help you. But be wise in whom you ask for advice. Gaining insight from a variety of people doesn't mean stopping anyone and everyone in hallways and grocery store lines and asking what they think about a given subject. Be selective. Talk to people who know and care about you, who know their field, and who bring experience deeper and broader than your own.

Take the same issue, problem, or project you considered on Day 24 to a good big-picture thinker who can give you insight on it. Formulate the questions you want to ask in advance and write them down before you meet.

*D*AY

27

A small man is made up of small thoughts.
VICTOR HUGO

If you want to be a big-picture thinker, you will have to go against the flow of the world. Society wants to keep people in boxes. Most people are married mentally to the status quo. They want what was, not what can be. They seek safety and simple answers. To think big-picture, you need to *give yourself permission to go a different way, to break new ground, to find new worlds to conquer.* And when your world does get bigger, you need to celebrate. Never forget there is more out there in the world than what you've experienced.

I grew up in a household where we believed anything was possible, and we celebrated the big picture. So it flabbergasted me when I had my first major experience with minds unalterably closed. In happened in 1969 when I took my first pastorate in rural Indiana. NASA was about to put a man on the moon for the first time in history, and I realized some members of the church did not believe it was really happening!

How important it is to keep learning, growing, and looking at the big picture! If you desire to be a good thinker, that's what you need to do.

What area of your thinking do you need to break out of the box that others would impose on you? Write a declaration giving yourself the permission to go a different way from the status quo.

DAY

28

To be able to concentrate for a considerable time is essential to difficult achievement.
BERTRAND RUSSELL

If you want to be successful, another thinking skill you need is to *unleash the potential of focused thinking*, because it can do several things for you:

Focused thinking can bring energy and power to almost anything, whether you're learning to develop a good curveball or to refine a manufacturing process. The greater the difficulty of a problem or issue, the more focus time is necessary to solve it.

Focused thinking also gives ideas time to develop. Try to be exhaustive in your thinking in order to generate as many ideas as possible, then shift to being selective.

Focused thinking brings clarity to the target or goal by removing distractions and mental clutter so you can concentrate on an issue. That's crucial, because if you don't know what the target is, how will you ever hit it?

Focused thinking will take you to the next level. No one achieves greatness by becoming a generalist. You don't hone a skill by diluting your attention to its development. No matter whether your goal is to sharpen your business plan, develop your subordinates, or solve personal problems, you need to focus.

On a scale of 1 to 10, with 1 being very scattered and 10 being very focused, how well do you focus your thinking? What is that lack of focus costing you?

DAY

29

Set priorities for your goals. . . . A major part of successful living lies in the ability to put first things first. Indeed, the reason most major goals are not achieved is that we spend our time doing second things first.

ROBERT J. McKAIN

Be selective, not exhaustive, in your focused thinking. First, take into account *your priorities*—for yourself, your family, and your team. There are many ways to determine priorities. If you know yourself well, begin by focusing on your strengths, the things that make the best use of your skills and God-given talents. You might also focus on what brings the highest return and reward. Do what you enjoy most and do best. You could use the 80/20 rule. Give 80 percent of your effort to the top 20 percent (most important) activities. Another way is to focus on exceptional opportunities that promise a huge return. It comes down to this: Give your attention to the areas that bear fruit.

Next, *discover your gifts*. If you do not have a good handle on your skills and talents, you need to figure out what your gifts are. Take a personality profile such as DISC or Myers-Briggs. Interview positive friends and family members to see where they think you shine. Reflect on past successes. If you're going to focus your thinking in your areas of strength, you need to know what they are.

What are the strengths in your life that you need to focus upon? What are your skills and talents? If you are unsure about your gifts, go online and take a DISC or Myers-Briggs test.

DAY

30

You will become as small as your controlling desire,
as great as your dominant aspiration.
JAMES ALLEN

If you want to achieve great things, you also need to focus your thinking on *developing your dream*. One wit said, "Too many minds are like plankton, a small sea plant that goes wherever the current takes it." If you're not sure of your dream, use your focused thinking time to help you discover it. If your thinking has returned to a particular area time after time, you may be able to discover your dream there. Give it more focused time and see what happens. Once you find your dream, move forward without second-guessing. Take the advice of Satchel Paige: "Don't look back—something might be gaining on you."

The younger you are, the more likely you will give your attention to many things. That's okay, because if you're young you're still getting to know yourself, your strengths and weaknesses. If you focus your thinking on only one thing and your aspirations change, you've wasted your best mental energy. As you get older and more experienced, the need to focus becomes more critical. The farther and higher you go, the more focused you can be—and need to be.

Who do you desire to be, and what do you desire to do with your life? Describe your dream. If you have not discovered it, schedule daily time to focus in on it until you know.

DAY

31

The real path to greatness, it turns out, requires simplicity
and diligence. It requires clarity, not instant illumination.
It demands each of us to focus on what is vital—
and to eliminate all of the extraneous distractions.

JIM COLLINS

Once you have a handle on what you should be thinking about, you must decide how to better focus on it. Start by *removing distractions.* How do you do it? First, by maintaining the discipline of practicing your priorities. Don't do easy things first or hard things first or urgent things first. Do first things first—the activities that give you the highest return. In that way, you keep the distractions to a minimum.

Second, *insulate yourself from distractions.* I've found that I need blocks of time to think without interruptions. I've mastered the art of making myself unavailable when necessary and going off to my "thinking place" so that I can work without interruptions. However, I am always aware of the tension between my need to remain accessible to others as a leader and my need to withdraw from them to think. My advice to you is to place value on and give attention to both. If you naturally withdraw, make sure to get out among people more often. If you're always on the go, remove yourself periodically so you can unleash the potential of focused thinking. And wherever you are . . . be there!

Look at your calendar and figure out when, where, and how to schedule daily thinking time. Also schedule a good block of time to think once a week. Put it on your calendar and treat it as you would any important appointment.

DAY

32

Concentration is the secret of strength in politics, in war, in trade, in short in all management of human affairs.
RALPH WALDO EMERSON

To better focus on what you should think about, *make time for focused thinking.* Because of the fast pace of our culture, people tend to multitask. But switching from task to task can cost you up to 40 percent efficiency. Focus on one task at a time, and reserve your best thinking time and energies on your number one priority. Put nonproductive time wasters on hold so that you can create thinking time for yourself.

Another way to help you concentrate on the things that matter is to *keep items of focus before you.* One way I do it is to ask my assistant, Linda Eggers, to keep high priorities in front of me. If an item needs attention or a decision, yet has not landed, I ask her to keep bringing it up, asking me about it, giving me additional information in reference to it. If I'm working on a presentation or the outline for a book, I'll keep a file or a page on my desk so that I see it every day as I work. That strategy has successfully helped me for forty years to stimulate and sharpen ideas.

Create visual reminders about the items currently on your plate that are most important, and put them where you will see them every day to jog your thinking.

DAY

33

Until input (thought) is linked to a goal (purpose)
there can be no intelligent accomplishment.

PAUL G. THOMAS

To better focus on what you should think about, *set goals*. The mind will not focus until it has clear objectives. But the purpose of goals is to focus your attention and give you direction, not to identify a final destination. Your goals should be:

- Clear enough to be kept in focus.
- Close enough to be achieved.
- Helpful enough to change lives.

Those guidelines will get you going. And be sure to write down your goals. If they're not written, I can almost guarantee that they're not focused enough. And if you really want to make sure they're focused, take the advice of David Belasco: "If you can't write your idea on the back of my business card, you don't have a clear idea."

Finally, the most accurate measure of whether you are making the best use of focused thinking is to *question your progress*. Ask yourself, "Is what I am doing getting me closer to my goals? Am I headed in a direction that helps me to fulfill my commitments, maintain my priorities, and realize my dreams?"

Dedicate this week's large block of thinking time to considering and writing down your current goals. Be sure they are aligned with your dreams.

DAY

34

Those who attain any excellence, commonly spend life in one pursuit; for excellence is not often gained upon easier terms.
SAMUEL JOHNSON

No one can go to the highest level and remain a generalist. My dad used to say, "Find the one thing you do well and don't do anything else." I've found that to do well at a few things, I've had to give up many things, such as:

- I can't know everyone. I'm a people person, but I have to restrict myself from spending time with lots of people and keep it to a strong inner circle of people.

- I can't do everything. Strive for excellence in a few things rather than a good performance in many.

- I can't go everywhere. Keeping the ridiculously demanding schedule of a conference speaker takes a toll that must be limited.

- I can't be well-rounded. I tell people, "Ninety-nine percent of everything in life I don't need to know about." I try to focus on the one percent that gives the highest return.

The earlier you embrace a willingness to give up some of the things you love in order to focus on what has the greatest impact, the sooner you can dedicate yourself to excellence in what matters most and unleash the potential of focused thinking.

What things do you need to give up so that you can dedicate yourself to excellence in what matters most?

DAY

35

The most valuable resource you bring to your work and to your firm is your creativity. More than what you get done, more than the role you play, more than your title, more than your "output"—it's your ideas that matter.

ANNETTE MOSER-WELLMAN

In one of my first college classes, after completing a profile that measured various natural talents, I remember being crushed by the results—I scored at the bottom of my class in creativity. I was studying to go into the ministry, which I knew required creativity for speaking and writing. What was I going to do? Well, I thought, if I don't have the innate ability to come up with creative thoughts myself, I'll mine the creative thoughts of others. By becoming a person always on the lookout for creative ideas, I learned to become a creative thinker myself.

As another thinking skill you must learn, creative thinking is pure gold, no matter what you do for a living. If you're not as creative as you would like to be, you can change your way of thinking, just as I did. Creative thinking isn't necessarily original thinking. Most often, creative thinking is a composite of other thoughts discovered along the way. Even the great artists learned from their masters, modeled their work on that of others, and gathered a host of ideas and styles to create their own work.

Describe how you have defined "creative thinking" up until now. Has your definition left you feeling inadequate and intimidated by others? How can you change that?

DAY

36

Imagination is more important than knowledge.
ALBERT EINSTEIN

Are you a creative thinker? Perhaps you're not even sure what I mean. Consider some characteristics that creative thinkers have in common. Creative thinkers:

- *Value ideas.* Creativity is about having lots of ideas. You will have ideas only if you value ideas.

- *Explore options*, because options provide the key to finding the best answer—not the only answer.

- *Embrace life's ambiguities* and often take delight in exploring those inconsistencies and gaps—or in using their imagination to fill them in.

- *Celebrate the offbeat.* Creativity, by its very nature, often explores off of the beaten path and goes against the grain.

- *Connect the unconnected.* Once you begin to think, you are free to collect. You ask yourself, *What material relates to this thought?* Once you have the material, you ask, *What ideas can make the thought better?* Then you ask, *What changes can make these ideas better?* Finally, you connect the ideas by positioning them in the right context to make the thought complete and powerful.

- *Don't fear failure*, because creativity equals failure.

On a scale of 1 to 10, with 1 being uncreative and 10 being highly creative, how creative is your thinking? Based on this list of characteristics, has your understanding of creativity changed? How so?

DAY

37

You can't use up creativity.
The more you use, the more you have.
MAYA ANGELOU

Creativity can improve a person's quality of life. Here are five specific things creative thinking has the potential to do for you:

- *Adds value to everything.* Creativity is being able to see what everybody else has seen and think what nobody else has thought so that you can do what nobody else has done. No matter what you are currently able to do, creativity can increase your capabilities.

- *Compounds* given enough time and focus. Creative thinking builds on itself and increases the creativity of the thinker.

- *Draws people to you and your ideas* because creativity is magnetic. Creativity is intelligence having fun. People admire intelligence, and they are always attracted to fun—so the combination is fantastic.

- *Helps you learn more.* If you are always actively seeking new ideas, you will learn. Creativity is teachability. It's seeing more solutions than problems.

- *Challenges the status quo.* The *status quo* and creativity are incompatible. Creativity and innovation always walk hand in hand.

Describe the difference that creativity has made in three of your past successes. If you were to increase your creativity, where do you think you would most benefit?

DAY

38

You cannot dig a hole in a different place
by digging the same hole deeper.
EDWARD DE BONO

So how do you find your creativity? How do you discover the joy of creative thought? I am going to give five ways to do it over the next five days.

First, *remove creativity killers*. Eliminate attitudes that devalue creative thinking, such as any of the following phrases:

I'm not creative.	It's never been done.
Follow the rules.	It can't be done.
Don't ask questions.	It didn't work for them.
Don't be different.	We tried that before.
Stay within the lines.	It's too much work.
Don't be foolish.	We don't have the time.
Be serious.	We don't have the money.
Think of your image.	Yes, but . . .
It's not practical.	Failure is final.

If you think you have a great idea, don't let anyone talk you out of it even if it sounds foolish. Don't let yourself or anyone else subject you to creativity killers. After all, you can't do something new and exciting if you force yourself to stay in the same old rut. Make a change.

Identify the creativity killers in your thinking. Begin by looking at my list. How will you work to break out of your "box" of limitations and overcome creativity killers so that you can explore ideas and options to experience breakthroughs?

DAY

39

*The uncreative mind can spot wrong answers,
but it takes a creative mind to spot wrong questions.*
SIR ANTONY JAY

The second way to find your creativity is to learn to *ask the right questions*. Wrong questions shut down the process of creative thinking. They direct thinkers down the same *old* path, or they chide them into believing that thinking isn't necessary at all.

To stimulate creative thinking, ask yourself questions such as . . .

- Why must it be done *this* way?
- What is the root problem?
- What are the underlying issues?
- What does this remind me of?
- What is the opposite?
- What metaphor or symbol helps to explain it?
- Why is it important?
- Who has a different perspective on this?
- What happens if we *don't* do it at all?

You get the idea—and you can probably come up with better questions yourself. If you want to think creatively, you must ask good questions and challenge the process.

Think about one of your ideas that you believe has great potential. Develop your own list of questions to stretch that idea and get outside of your box.

DAY

40

*A new idea is delicate. It can be killed by a sneer or a yawn;
it can be stabbed to death by a quip and worried to
death by a frown on the right man's brow.*

CHARLIE BROWER

The third way to find your creativity is to *develop a creative environment*. Negative environments kill great ideas. A creative environment is like a greenhouse where ideas get seeded, sprout up, and flourish. A creative environment:

- Encourages and openly rewards creativity.
- Places a high value on trust among team members and individuality, because creativity always risks failure.
- Embraces and celebrates those who are creative.
- Focuses on innovation, not just invention. Creative people say, "Give me a good idea and I'll give you a better idea!"
- Places a high value on options, which bring opportunities.
- Is willing to let people go outside the lines and challenge boundaries.
- Appreciates the power and promotes the freedom of a dream.

The more creativity-friendly you can make your environment, the more potential it has to become creative.

Does your environment naturally foster creativity or tend to shut it down? Describe it. What can you do to make it friendlier to creativity?

DAY

*Great discoveries and achievements
invariably involve the cooperation of many minds.*
ALEXANDER GRAHAM BELL

The fourth way to find your creativity is to *spend time with other creative people*. Creativity is contagious. Have you ever noticed what happens during a good brainstorming session? One person throws out an idea. Another person uses it as a springboard to discover another idea. Then somebody grabs hold of it and takes it to a whole new level. The interplay of ideas can be electric.

What if the place you work has an environment hostile to creativity, and you possess little ability to change it? One possibility is to change jobs. But what if you desire to keep working there despite the negative environment? Your best option is to find a way to spend time with other creative people.

It's a fact that you begin to think like the people you spend a lot of time with. I have a strong group of creative individuals with whom I make sure to spend regular time. When I leave them, I always feel energized, I'm full of ideas, and I see things differently. They truly are indispensable to my life. The more time you can spend with creative people engaging in creative activities, the more creative you will become.

Are there creative people within your workplace? If so, go out of your way to spend regular time with them. If not, identify creative people outside your workplace and figure out how to spend time with them.

DAY

42

If you obey all the rules . . . you will miss all the fun.
KATHARINE HEPBURN

The fifth way to find your creativity is to *get out of your box*. While I don't think it's necessary to break all the rules (many are in place to protect us), I do think it's unwise to follow rules blindly or to allow self-imposed limitations to hinder us. Creative thinkers are out-of-the-box people. They know that they must repeatedly break out of the "box" of their own history and personal limitations in order to experience creative breakthroughs.

The most effective way to help yourself get out of the box is to expose yourself to new paradigms. One way you can do that is by traveling to new places. Explore other cultures, countries, and traditions. Find out how people very different from you live and think. Another is to read on new subjects. I'm naturally curious and love to learn, but I still have a tendency to read books only on my favorite subjects, such as leadership. I sometimes have to force myself to read books that broaden my thinking, because I know it's worth it. If you want to break out of your own box, get into somebody else's. Read broadly.

What country might you visit on your next vacation in order to immerse yourself in a different culture? What book out of your area of expertise will you read now to stretch your mind and get you outside of your box?

DAY

43

The first responsibility of a leader is to define reality.
MAX DEPREE

Early in my career, I was an idealistic thinker. I went out of my way to avoid too much realistic thinking because I thought that always having to consider "What's the worst-case scenario" was too negative and would interfere with my creative thinking. But I've found that cultivating the skill to be a realistic thinker will not undermine your faith in people, nor will it lessen your ability to see and seize opportunities. Instead, realistic thinking:

- *Minimizes downside risk.* Actions always have consequences; realistic thinking helps you recognize and consider what those consequences could be so you can plan for them.

- *Gives you a target and game plan.* Remember: Hope is not a strategy. As you face reality, you can begin to define a target and develop a game plan and then also begin to simplify practices and procedures, which results in better efficiency.

- *Is a catalyst for change.* Staring reality in the face makes a person recognize the need for change. Change alone doesn't bring growth but you cannot have growth without change.

On a scale of 1 to 10, with 1 being idealistic and 10 being realistic, how would you rate yourself when it comes to realistic thinking? Do you avoid considering the "worst-case scenario"? If so, what is the problem with this thinking? How can you change it?

DAY

44

The value of a good idea is in using it.
THOMAS EDISON

If you're a naturally optimistic person, as I am, you may not possess a great desire to become a more realistic thinker, but it is a skill you must learn. Continuing with ideas in yesterday's reading, here are five more benefits I have found to realistic thinking:

- *Provides security.* Any time you have thought through the worst that can happen and you have developed contingency plans to meet it, you become more confident and secure, knowing you are unlikely to be surprised.

- *Gives you credibility.* Leaders who think realistically and plan accordingly position their organizations to win. That gives their people confidence in them.

- *Provides a foundation to build on* and to make your ideas usable by taking away the "wish" factor.

- *Is a friend to those in trouble.* It gives you something concrete to fall back on during times of trouble. Certainty in the midst of uncertainty brings stability.

- *Brings the dream to fruition.* If you don't take a realistic look at your dream—and what it will take to accomplish it—you will never achieve it.

In what areas of your life can you most benefit from realistic thinking? What steps will you take today to move your thinking in that direction?

DAY

45

Men occasionally stumble over the truth, but most pick themselves up and hurry off as if nothing has happened.
WINSTON CHURCHILL

If you are naturally optimistic rather than realistic like me, you will have to take concrete steps to improve your thinking in this area. Over the next three days, I will present five things I do to improve my realistic thinking.

People tend to exaggerate their successes and minimize their failures or deficiencies. They live according to Ruckert's Law, believing there is nothing so small that it can't be blown out of proportion, whether it's on their résumé or a sales presentation. However, when exposed as a lie and lack of integrity, it wipes out one's credibility.

First, I could not develop as a realistic thinker until I *developed an appreciation for truth*. And that means learning to look at and enjoy truth. Television journalist Ted Koppel observed, "Our society finds truth too strong a medicine to digest undiluted. In its purest form, truth is not a polite tap on the shoulder. It is a howling reproach." In other words, the truth will set you free—but first it will make you angry! If you want to become a realistic thinker, however, you need to get comfortable dealing with the truth and face up to it.

To get the truth about yourself, ask five astute people (friends, coworkers, your spouse, your supervisor, etc.) to talk to you about your three greatest strengths and three greatest weaknesses. Write down their comments, give them some thought, and assess how your strengths and weaknesses impact your effectiveness.

DAY

46

When you approach a problem, strip yourself of preconceived opinions and prejudice, assemble and learn the facts of the situation, make the decision that seems to you to be the most honest, and then stick to it.

CHESTER BOWLES

The second step to improve your realistic thinking is to *do your homework*. You must first get the facts. It doesn't matter how sound your thinking is if it's based on faulty data or assumptions or an absence of facts. You can also find out what others have done in similar circumstances. Why not learn all that you can from good thinkers who have faced similar situations in the past?

Next, there's nothing like taking the time to really *examine the pros and cons* of an issue to give you a strong dose of reality. It rarely comes down to simply choosing the course of action with the greatest number of pros, because all pros and cons do not carry equal weight. But rather, it helps you to dig into the facts, examine an issue from many angles, and really count the cost of a possible course of action.

After looking at the pros and cons and examining worst-case scenarios that make you aware of any gaps between what you desire and what really is, you can maximize realistic thinking to *align your resources with your objectives*. After all, that's what resources are for.

Consider a current problem or project and take the following two steps: Do your homework and write out an overview of it. Next, describe the pros and cons of the challenge you're facing. Then proceed to tomorrow's action and continue on with two more steps.

DAY

47

*Deliberate with caution, but act with decision;
and yield with graciousness or oppose with firmness.*
CHARLES HOLE

The essence of realistic thinking is *discovering, picturing, and examining the worst-case scenarios.* Ask yourself questions such as,

- What if sales fall short of projections?
- What if revenue hits rock bottom?
- What if we don't win the account?
- What if our best player gets hurt?
- What if all the colleges reject my application?
- What if the market goes belly up?
- What if the volunteers quit or nobody shows up?

You get the idea. The point is that you need to think about worst-case possibilities whether you're running a business, leading a department, pastoring a church, coaching a team, or planning your future. Your goal isn't to expect the worst, just to be ready for it in case it happens. That way, you give yourself the best chance for a positive result—no matter what.

Continuing with yesterday's action, having done your homework and worked through the pros and cons, now describe the worst-case scenario if things go wrong and align your thinking and your resources accordingly. Go through all four steps before you take action.

DAY

48

*What we like to think of ourselves and what we
really are rarely have much in common.*
STEPHEN KING

What is your natural bent? Is it toward optimism or
realism? Take a look at the following statements and see
which one best describes you.

1. I do not engage in realistic thinking.
2. I do not like realistic thinking.
3. I will let someone else do realistic thinking.
4. I will do realistic thinking only after I am in trouble.
5. I will do realistic thinking before I am in trouble.
6. I will continually make realistic thinking part of my
   life.
7. I will encourage my key leaders to do the same.
8. I will make realistic thinking the foundation of our
   business.
9. I derive certainty and security from realistic thinking.
10. I rely heavily on facts and often make judgments
    according to the worst-case scenario.

These statements represent my growth in realistic
thinking. The lower the number of the statement you
picked, the more you need to grow in realistic thinking.

What practical
steps will
you take to
improve your
ability to think
realistically?

....

....

....

....

....

....

....

....

....

....

....

....

....

....

....

....

....

....

....

....

....

....

DAY

49

The man who is prepared has his battle half fought.
MIGUEL DE CERVANTES

When you hear the words *strategic thinking*, business and marketing plans or military campaigns might come to mind, but strategic thinking is a learned skill that can make a positive impact on any area of life. I use strategic thinking to help me to plan, to become more efficient, to maximize my strengths, and to find the most direct path toward achieving any objective. You should adopt it as one of your thinking tools because:

Strategic thinking simplifies the difficult by breaking things down into manageable sizes and helping you simplify the management of everyday life. I do that by using systems, which are nothing more than good strategies repeated, and I use them for everything from my system to file quotes, stories, and articles to the seven instructional messages I listen to in the car every week. Anything becomes simpler when it has a plan!

Strategic thinking prompts you to ask the right questions in order to break down complex and difficult issues and begin formulating a strategic plan. What is our next step? Why? Do we have the right people in the right positions of responsibility? What will it cost, and can we afford it?

On a scale of 1 to 10, with 1 being "fly by the seat of your pants" and 10 being highly strategic, how do you rate yourself as a strategic thinker? Write down three examples of where you were strategic in your thinking and the positive results it netted.

DAY

50

Saddle your dreams before you ride 'em.
MARY WEBB

I have unleashed the power of strategic thinking to be able to accomplish so much. Here are a few more reasons you should adopt it as one of your thinking tools:

Strategic thinking prompts customization and precision. It helps you to match the strategy to the problem, because strategy isn't a one-size-fits-all proposition. Sloppy or generalized thinking is an enemy of achievement.

Strategic thinking prepares you today for an uncertain tomorrow. It is the bridge that links where you are to where you want to be. It gives direction and credibility today and increases your potential for success tomorrow.

Strategic thinking reduces the margin of error. It lines up your actions with your objectives and betters the odds that you will be going in the right direction.

Strategic thinking gives you influence with others. In whatever kind of activity you're involved, the one with the plan is the one with the power. If you practice strategic thinking, others will listen to and want to follow you.

What specific areas of your life would benefit most from strategic thinking? What changes are needed to make that happen?

DAY

51

Yard by yard, life is hard; but inch by inch, it's a cinch.
ROBERT SCHULLER

To become a better strategic thinker able to formulate and implement plans that will achieve the desired objective, over the next four days take the following guidelines to heart:

Break down the issues into smaller, more manageable parts so that you can focus on them more effectively. How you do it, whether it's by function, timetable, responsibility, purpose, or some other method, is not as important as just doing it. When Henry Ford created the assembly line, he said, "Nothing is particularly hard if you divide it into small jobs."

Ask "why" before "how." Instead of asking *how* to solve a problem or plan a way to meet an objective, you should first ask *why*. If you jump right into problem solving mode, how are you going to know all the issues? Asking *why* helps you to think about all the reasons for decisions. It helps you to open your mind to possibilities and opportunities. The size of an opportunity often determines the level of resources and effort that you must invest. Big opportunities allow for big decisions. If you jump to *how* too quickly, you might miss that.

Write down a major objective for which you are currently planning. Next, write "why" questions concerning your objective. Then break it down into smaller parts. Note any opportunities that you had not seen before.

DAY

52

Strategy is first trying to understand where you sit in today's world. Not where you wish you were or where you hoped you would be, but where you are. Then it's trying to understand where you want to be five years out. Finally, it's assessing the realistic chances of getting from here to there.

JACK WELCH

To release the power of strategic thinking, here are two more guidelines to help you formulate and implement plans that will achieve the desired objective:

Identify the real issues and objectives. Too many people rush to solutions, and as a result they end up solving the wrong problem. You avoid that by asking probing questions in an effort to expose the real issues. Begin by asking, *what else could be the real issue?* Challenge all of your assumptions. Collect information even after you think you've identified the issue. Don't jump to a conclusion before you gather enough information to begin identifying the real issue.

Review your resources. A strategy that doesn't take into account resources is doomed to failure. How much time and money do you have? What kinds of materials, supplies, inventory, or other assets do you have? What liabilities or obligations will come into play? Which people on the team can make an impact? Figure out what resources you have at your disposal.

Continuing with yesterday's thinking about a major objective for which you are currently planning, identify and write down the real issues and objectives, then write a review of your resources.

DAY

53

Reduce your plan to writing. . . .
The moment you complete this, you will have
definitely given concrete form to the intangible desire.
NAPOLEON HILL

My fifth guideline to equip you to become a better strategic thinker is to *develop your plan.* How you approach the planning process depends greatly on your profession and the size of the challenge, so it's difficult to recommend many specifics. However, Rolf Smith, the author of *The 7 Levels of Change*, outlines seven kinds of change, which may prompt you in your planning process:

Level 1: Effectiveness—Doing the right things
Level 2: Efficiency—Doing the right things right
Level 3: Improving—Doing things better
Level 4: Cutting—Doing away with things
Level 5: Adapting—Doing things other people are doing
Level 6: Different—Doing things no one else is doing
Level 7: Impossible—Doing things that can't be done

No matter how you go about planning, start with the obvious. When you tackle an issue or plan that way, it brings unity and consensus to the team, because everyone sees those things. Obvious elements build mental momentum and initiate creativity and intensity.

Continuing with yesterday's thinking about a major objective for which you are currently planning, start with the obvious and develop your plan.

DAY

54

*The will to win is worthless if you
do not have the will to prepare.*
THANE YOST

I have two more guidelines to become a better strategic thinker able to formulate and implement plans that will achieve the desired objective:

Put the right people in the right place. It's critical that you include your team as part of your strategic thinking. Before you can implement your plan, you must make sure that you have the right people in place. Even the best strategic thinking won't help if you don't take into account the people part of the equation. Everything comes together, however, when you put together all three elements: the right people, place, and plan.

Keep repeating the process. My friend Olan Hendrix remarked, "Strategic thinking is like showering; you have to keep doing it." If you expect to solve any major problem once, you're in for disappointment. Little things, such as filing or shopping systematically, can be won easily through systems and personal discipline. But major issues need major strategic thinking time. If you want to be an effective strategic thinker, you need to become a continuous strategic thinker.

Continuing with yesterday's thinking about a major objective for which you are currently planning, write a review of whether you have the right people in the right places to help you implement your plan. If you don't, what step will you take to make that happen?

....

....

....

....

....

....

....

....

....

....

....

....

....

....

....

....

....

....

DAY

55

Nothing is so embarrassing as watching someone do something that you said could not be done.

SAM EWING

When filmmaker George Lucas set out with his vision for the movie *Star Wars*, he was told that it was technically impossible, but he believed it could be done. After two years of inventing and assembling the technology needed to make the impossible possible, *Star Wars* became the most technically innovative and profitable movie in history at that time. Lucas exemplifies the fact that people who develop the skill of possibility thinking are capable of accomplishing tasks that seem impossible because they believe in solutions. You should become a possibility thinker because:

Possibility thinking increases your possibilities. When you believe you can do something difficult—and you succeed—many doors open for you, as they did for George Lucas and his studio.

Possibility thinking draws opportunities and people to you. If Lucas had not believed *Star Wars* was possible and made the film, few of his other movies would have been made and some of the most talented people in the world would not have came to work for him at his studio. People who think big attract big people to them. If you want to achieve big things, you need to become a possibility thinker.

If you've had your dreams put down in the past, you need to recapture your possibility thinking. What was the thing in your heart that you really wanted to do? Rekindle that thought, write it down, explore it, and do some dreaming with it.

DAY

56

*Big thinkers are specialists in creating positive,
forward-looking, optimistic pictures in their
own minds and in the minds of others.*

DAVID J. SCHWARTZ

If your thinking runs toward pessimism, let me ask
you a question: How many highly successful people do
you know who are continually negative? None, I bet! Here
are five more benefits from learning the skill of possibility
thinking:

- *Increases others' possibilities.* That happens, in part,
  because possibility thinking is contagious. You can't
  help but become more confident and think bigger
  when you're around possibility thinkers.

- *Allows you to dream big dreams,* no matter what your
  profession, and because you believe in possibilities,
  you put yourself in position to achieve them.

- *Makes it possible to rise above average.* Every time you
  remove the label of impossible from a task, you raise
  your potential from average to off the charts.

- *Gives you energy,* because you invest yourself in what
  you believe can succeed.

- *Keeps you from giving up,* because if you believe you will
  succeed, you have already won much of the battle.

Continuing with yesterday's thought, what do you really want to do now? What is your dream? If you didn't fear failure or being laughed at, what would you start doing today? Write that down.

DAY

57

*I have learned to use the word "impossible"
with the greatest of caution.*
WERNHER VON BRAUN

People with an it-can't-be-done mindset have two choices. They can expect the worst and continually experience it; or they can change their thinking. To put possibility thinking to work for you, follow the suggestions I make over the next three days:

Stop focusing on the impossibilities. When you automatically start listing all the things that can go wrong or all the reasons something can't be done, stop yourself and say, "Don't go there." Yes, at some point you will want to look at ideas realistically, but that's not where you should start. Instead, ask, "What's right about this?" That will help to get the ball rolling toward possibility thinking.

Stay away from the "experts," who often shoot down other people's dreams. Consider that in 1943, Thomas Watson, chairman of IBM, said, "I think there is a world market for about five computers." Instead, heed the words of John Andrew Holmes, who asserted, "Never tell a young person that something cannot be done. God may have been waiting centuries for somebody ignorant enough of the impossible to do that thing."

Continuing with yesterday's thought about what your dream is today, think about what's right with your idea. Write down your thoughts.

DAY

*Make your plans as fantastic as you like,
because twenty-five years from now, they will seem
mediocre. Make your plans ten times as great as you first
planned, and twenty-five years from now you will wonder
why you did not make them fifty times as great.*

HENRY CURTIS

Two of the best ways to cultivate a possibility mind-set are found in the following suggestions:

Look for possibilities in every situation. Don't just refuse to let yourself be negative. Look for positive possibilities despite the circumstances. Every situation can be seen as potentially better than it is at present. Possibility thinking is possible even in negative situations. Sam Walton was a master of gathering positive possibilities from the worst of competitors' stores and implementing them into Wal-Mart. All it takes to find the possibility in every situation is the right attitude, and anybody can cultivate that.

Dream one size bigger. Most people dream too small. They don't think big enough. People need BHAGs—big hairy audacious goals—as the authors of *Built to Last* maintain. If you push yourself to dream more expansively, to make your goals at least a step beyond what makes you comfortable, you will be forced to grow. And it will set you up to believe in greater possibilities.

Take a present situation that you are dealing with and write down the possibilities it affords. Then dream one size bigger. What would that look like?

DAY

59

Some men see things as they are and say, "Why?"
I dream of things that never were and say, "Why not?"
GEORGE BERNARD SHAW

Here are two more ways to cultivate a possibility mind-set:

Question the status quo. Most people want their lives to keep improving, yet they value peace and stability at the same time. People often forget that you can't improve and still stay the same. Growth means change. Change requires challenging the status quo. If you want greater possibilities, you can't settle for what you have now. As you begin to explore greater possibilities for yourself, your organization, or your family—and others challenge you for it—take comfort in knowing that achievers refuse to accept the status quo.

Find inspiration by studying the lives of great achievers. Look for people with the attitude of George Lucas, whom I used as an example of a possibility thinker.

I know possibility thinking isn't in style with some people. So call it what you like: the will to succeed, belief in yourself, confidence in your ability, faith. It's really true: People who believe they can't, don't. But if you believe you can, you can! That's the power of possibility thinking.

This week, read a biography of someone you admire. Make notes concerning how that person harnessed the energy of possibility thinking. Then write three to five principles or practices from that person's life that you can apply to your own.

DAY

60

*To doubt everything or to believe
everything are two equally convenient solutions;
both dispense with the necessity of reflection.*
JULES HENRI POINCARÉ

Reflective thinking is another thinking skill you need to learn. It's been a major part of my life for decades. I'm constantly reflecting and reviewing my life so that I can keep growing and celebrating victories. At the end of every day, I ask myself three questions: *What did I learn today? What should I share? What must I do?* Every Sunday night, I review the previous week, reflecting on the effectiveness of the weekend's activities and evaluating everything in order to prepare for the coming week. I also review my calendar every month and look at the forty days ahead, and at the end of each December, I reflect on the past year.

As I go through these processes, my goal is to reflect on how I spent my time so that I might learn from my successes and mistakes, discover what I should try to repeat, and determine what I should change. It is always a valuable exercise. By mentally visiting past situations, you can think with greater understanding. Reflective thinking is like the Crock-Pot of the mind. It encourages your thoughts to simmer until they're done.

On a scale of 1 to 10, with 1 meaning you never look back to reflect and 10 meaning you are highly intentional about being reflective, how do you rate yourself as a reflective thinker? Write down three examples of where you were reflective in your thinking and the positive results it netted.

DAY

61

We ought not to look back unless it is to derive useful lessons from past errors and for the purpose of profiting by dearly bought experience.

GEORGE WASHINGTON

The pace of our society does not encourage reflective thinking. Most people would rather act than think. Now, don't get me wrong. I'm a person of action, but I'm also a reflective thinker because:

Reflective thinking gives you true perspective on your experiences. You are able to evaluate their value and their timing. And you are able to gain a new appreciation for things that before went unnoticed.

Reflective thinking gives emotional integrity to your thought life. It enables you to distance yourself from the intense emotions of past experiences and see them with fresh eyes. You can see the thrills of the past in the light of emotional maturity and examine tragedies in the light of truth and logic. That process can help you stop carrying around a bunch of negative emotional baggage.

Reflective thinking turns your experience into insights. Experiences alone do not add value to a life; it's the insight people gain because of their experience. An experience becomes valuable when reflective thinking informs or equips us to meet new experiences.

Write down one situation where you acted too quickly and could have enjoyed a better result if you used reflective thinking. What lessons can you glean from that experience?

DAY

62

We should be careful to get out of an experience all the wisdom that is in it—not like the cat that sits down on a hot stove lid. She will never sit down on a hot stove lid again—and that is well; but also she will never sit down on a cold one anymore.

MARK TWAIN

Here are two more valuable reasons to become a reflective thinker:

Reflective thinking increases your confidence in decision-making. It helps to diffuse the doubts that surround snap judgments, and it also gives you confidence for the next decision. Once you've reflected on an issue, you don't have to repeat every step of the thinking process when you're faced with it again.

Reflective thinking clarifies the big picture. It encourages us to go back and spend time pondering what we have done and seen and helps put ideas and experiences into a more accurate context. If a person who loses his job reflects on what happened, he may see a pattern of events that led to his dismissal and what things were his responsibility. He may realize that in the larger scheme of things, he's better off in his new position because it better fits his skills and desires. Without reflection, it can be very difficult to see that big picture.

Think about a current situation that you have not yet reflected on. Give it some thinking time to lead to better results. Write out the observations you discover while reflecting.

DAY

The unexamined life is not worth living.
SOCRATES

If you are like most people in our culture today, you probably do very little reflective thinking. If that's the case, it may be holding you back more than you think. Take to heart the following suggestions to increase your ability to think reflectively:

Set aside time for reflection. For most people, reflection and self-examination doesn't come naturally. It can be a fairly uncomfortable activity for a variety of reasons: you may have a hard time staying focused; you may find the process dull, or you may not like spending a lot of time thinking about emotionally difficult issues. But if you don't carve out the time for it, you are unlikely to do any reflective thinking.

Remove yourself from distractions. As much as any other kind of thinking, reflection requires solitude. Distraction and reflection simply don't mix. One of the reasons I've been able to accomplish much and keep growing personally is that I've not only set aside time to reflect, but I've separated myself from distractions for short blocks of time. The place doesn't matter—as long as you remove yourself from distractions and interruptions.

Create a daily reflection time to help you learn from the events of your day and to capture your ideas. Put it in your calendar and practice the discipline of daily reflective thinking for the next twenty-one days.

DAY

64

Successful people ask better questions,
and as a result, they get better answers.
TONY ROBBINS

The value you receive from reflecting will depend on whether you *ask the right questions*. The better the questions, the more gold you will mine from your thinking. When I reflect, I think in terms of my values, relationships, and experiences. Here are some sample questions from each area:

Personal Growth: What have I learned today that will help me grow? How can I apply it to my life? When should I apply it?

Inner Circle: Have I spent enough time with my key players? What can I do to help them be more successful? In what areas can I mentor them?

Successes: What went right? Did I create it? Is there a principle I can learn from the experience?

How you organize your reflection time is up to you. The main thing is to create questions that work for you, and write down any significant thoughts that come to you during the reflection time.

Create your own set of questions to ask yourself during your reflective thinking times. Begin by creating general questions to be used after any event or meeting. Then create more specific questions related to your values and relationships.

DAY

65

*Follow effective action with quiet reflection. From the
quiet reflection will come even more effective action.*
PETER DRUCKER

Regularly reviewing your calendar or journal is another
reflective thinking tool. Calendars and journals remind
you of how you've spent your time, show you whether your
activities match your priorities, and help you see whether
you are making progress. They also offer you an opportunity to recall activities that you might not have had the
time to reflect on previously. Some of the most valuable
thoughts you've ever had may have been lost because you
didn't give yourself the reflection time you needed.

Writing down the good thoughts that come out of
your reflective thinking has value, but nothing helps you
to grow like *putting your thoughts into action.* To do that,
you must be intentional. Record and review all the take-
aways you get while reading a book, listening to a pod-
cast, or attending a conference or seminar. Putting your
thoughts into action can change your life.

Ultimately, reflective thinking has three main values: it
gives me perspective within context, it allows me to continually connect with my journey, and it provides counsel and
direction concerning my future. Few things in life can help
me learn and improve the way reflective thinking can.

Set aside a block of time to review your appointments and to-do lists from the past month. Write down where you spent your time and whether you did so wisely. As you reflect, record lessons learned, insights to be filed, and action points to be completed.

DAY

66

*The difficulty lies not so much in developing
new ideas as in escaping from the old ones.*
JOHN MAYNARD KEYNES

For years, popular thinking among physicians held that the best predictor of potential heart attacks was high cholesterol. Cardiologist Paul Ridker challenged popular thinking to find out why about half of all heart attacks occur in people with normal cholesterol levels. Despite many naysayers, he discovered that C-reactive protein (CRP) is present in the blood of those with a high risk of heart attack and that tracking CRP better predicts heart problems than checking for elevated LDL cholesterol.

Successful people question the acceptance of popular thinking because *popular thinking sometimes means not thinking.* Unfortunately, many people try to live life the easy way. They don't want to do the hard work of thinking or pay the price of success. It's easier to do what other people do and hope that they thought it out.

Another reason is that *popular thinking brings only average results.* Remember: Popular = Normal = Average. It's the least of the best and the best of the least. We limit our success when we adopt popular thinking. It represents putting in the least energy to just get by. You must reject common thinking if you want to achieve uncommon results.

On a scale of 1 to 10, with 1 being popular thinking and 10 being uncommon thinking, how do you rate yourself as a thinker? Write down three examples of where you questioned popular thinking and the positive results it netted.

DAY

67

We must discard the idea that past routine,
past ways of doing things, are probably the best ways.
On the contrary, we must assume that there is
probably a better way to do almost everything.
DONALD M. NELSON

You should also question the acceptance of popular thinking because *it offers false hope.* Just because a lot of people are doing something does not make it a good idea. Because most people accept it does not mean it represents fairness, equality, compassion, and sensitivity. Popular thinking says buy now with a credit card, pay later, and so people pay and pay. Many promises of popular thinking ring hollow.

Popular thinking is also slow to embrace change. It loves the status quo. It puts its confidence in the idea of the moment and holds on to it with all its might, resisting change and dampening innovation. Homer Hickam grew up in a coal mining town in West Virginia, where popular thinking said every young man was destined to work in the mines. Homer wanted to build rockets and become an astronaut. He fought an uphill battle to break free from the town and his father's wishes, received his education from Virginia Tech, and became an engineer at NASA, training astronauts. Fighting popular thinking may be a slow process—but it's a worthwhile one.

Where in your life are you on autopilot? Where are you conforming to popular thinking when you shouldn't? Write a list. Then pick one example and plan what you will do to change your thinking.

DAY

68

I'm not an answering machine.
I'm a questioning machine. If we have all the answers,
how come we're in such a mess?

DOUGLAS CARDINAL

Popular thinking has often proved to be wrong and limiting. Questioning it isn't necessarily hard, once you cultivate the habit of doing so. Begin by doing the following:

Think before you follow. Many individuals follow others almost automatically. Sometimes they do so because they desire to take the path of least resistance. Other times they fear rejection. Or they believe there's wisdom in doing what everyone else does. But if you want to succeed, you need to think about what's best, not what's popular. You need to be willing to be unpopular and go outside of the norm. Remind yourself that unpopular thinking is required for all progress, contains the seeds of vision and opportunity, and is largely underrated, unrecognized, and misunderstood.

One of the ways to embrace innovation and change is to learn to *appreciate thinking that is different from your own.* To do that, you must continually expose yourself to people with different backgrounds, education levels, professional experiences, personal interests, etc. If you spend time with people who think out of the box, you're more likely to challenge popular thinking and break new ground.

Browse biographies and memoirs to find a book written by or about someone you ordinarily would not relate to or someone with experience in an area unfamiliar to you. As you read it, take notes on how that person thought differently and what you can learn from him or her.

DAY

69

*The Wright brothers flew right through
the smoke screen of impossibilities.*
CHARLES F. KETTERING

If you are going to question popular thinking, you will have to *continually question your own thinking.* Any time we find a way of thinking that works, one of our greatest temptations is to go back to it repeatedly, even if it no longer works well. The greatest enemy to tomorrow's success is sometimes today's success. In your organization, if you were involved in putting into place what currently exists, it's likely that you will resist change—even change for the better. That's why it's important to challenge your own thinking. If you're too attached to your own thinking and how everything is done now, nothing will change for the better.

Most people are more satisfied with old problems than committed to finding new solutions. So when was the last time you did something for the first time? Do you avoid taking risks or trying new things? One of the best ways to get out of the rut of your own thinking is to innovate—*to try new things in new ways.* You can do that in little, everyday ways.

Shake up your routine this week by driving to work a different way each day. Or ask a different colleague to help you with a familiar project.

DAY

70

All too often, on the long road up, young leaders become servants of what is rather than shapers of what might be.
JOHN GARDNER

When it comes right down to it, popular thinking is comfortable. It's like an old recliner adjusted to all the owner's idiosyncrasies. The problem with most old recliners is that we lose perspective about what they really look like. If we saw them with fresh eyes, we'd agree that it's time to get new ones!

If you want to reject popular thinking in order to embrace achievement, you'll have to *get used to being uncomfortable.* It's like swimming upstream. I know, because I've worked at it most of my life. Often when I went along with what everyone else believed, down deep I knew I was not reaching my potential. When I did find the courage to go against the flow, it allowed me to break new ground and reap good results. And it allowed me to help others.

If you reject popular thinking and make decisions based upon what works best and what is right rather than what is commonly accepted, know this: In your early years you won't be as wrong as people think you are. In your later years, you won't be as right as people think you are. And all through the years, you will be better than you thought you could be.

To get used to being uncomfortable, do something every day for the next week in a way different from what you're used to. For instance, arrange your day in an order different from how you usually do. Or listen to music that's different from what you generally like. Shake up your mind!

*D*AY

71

None of us is as smart as all of us.
KEN BLANCHARD

Good thinkers, especially those who are also good leaders, understand the power of shared thinking. They know that when they value the thoughts and ideas of others, they receive the compounding results of shared thinking and accomplish more than they ever could on their own. They understand the following:

Shared thinking is faster than solo thinking. We live in a truly fast-paced world. To function at its current rate of speed, we can't go it alone. Working with others is like giving yourself a shortcut. If you want to learn a new skill quickly, you can always learn more quickly from someone with experience—whether you're trying to learn how to use a new software package, develop your golf swing, or cook a new dish.

Shared thinking is more innovative than solo thinking. We tend to think of great thinkers and innovators as soloists, but the greatest innovative thinking doesn't occur in a vacuum. Shared thinking leads to greater innovation, whether you look at the work of researchers Marie and Pierre Curie or songwriters John Lennon and Paul McCartney. If you combine your thoughts with the thoughts of others, you will come up with thoughts you've never had!

On a scale of 1 to 10, with 1 indicating that you never ask others for input and 10 indicating that you nearly always invite others to share their ideas, how do you rate yourself as a shared thinker? Write down three examples of where you shared thinking and the positive results it netted.

DAY

72

To accept good advice is but to increase one's own ability.
JOHANN WOLFGANG VON GOETHE

As much as we wish we know it all, we all have our blind spots and areas of inexperience. When I first started out as a pastor, I had dreams and energy, but little experience. To try to overcome that, I attempted to get several high-profile pastors to share their thinking with me. When one said yes, I'd visit him. I listened intently, took careful notes, and absorbed everything I could. Those experiences changed my life.

Shared thinking brings more maturity than solo thinking. You've had experiences I haven't, and I've had experiences you haven't. Put us together and we bring a broader range of personal history—and therefore maturity—to the table. If you don't have the experience you need, connect with people who do.

Shared thinking is also stronger than solo thinking. Two horses pulling together are stronger than either is individually. But did you know that when they pull together, they can move more weight than the sum of what they can move individually? A synergy comes from working together. That same kind of energy comes into play when people think together.

Continuing with yesterday's thought, if you gave yourself a score lower than a seven, do some soul searching and write down why you feel reluctant to include others in the process. Shared thinking is the easiest kind of thinking to improve, because it's based on attitude, not talent.

DAY

73

He that is taught only by himself has a fool for a master.
BEN JONSON

Because shared thinking is stronger than solo thinking, *shared thinking yields a higher return of value.* That happens because of the compounding action of shared thinking. But it also offers other benefits. The personal return you receive from shared thinking and experiences can be great. Clarence Francis sums up the benefits in the following observation: "I sincerely believe that the word *relationships* is the key to the prospect of a decent world. It seems abundantly clear that every problem you will have—in your family, in your work, in our nation, or in this world—is essentially a matter of relationships, of interdependence."

I believe that every great idea begins with three or four good ideas, and that *shared thinking is the only way to have great thinking.* When I was in school, teachers rarely put the emphasis on working together to come up with good answers. Yet all the answers improve when they make the best use of everyone's thinking. If we each have one thought, and together we have two thoughts, we always have the potential for a great thought.

Pick a difficult challenge you are currently facing, and assemble a group of people to help you think about it. Define and analyze the problem together, and then brainstorm solutions together.

DAY

74

Listening to advice often accomplishes far more than heeding it.
MALCOLM FORBES

Some people naturally participate in shared thinking. Any time they see a problem, they think, *Who do I know who can help with this?* Leaders tend to be that way. So do extroverts. However, you don't have to be either of those to benefit from shared thinking. To help you improve your ability to harness shared thinking, first, *value the ideas of others.* If you don't, your hands will be tied.

How do you know if you truly want input from others? Ask yourself these questions:

Am I emotionally secure? People who lack confidence and worry about their status, position, or power tend to reject the ideas of others, protect their turf, and keep people at bay. It takes a secure person to consider others' ideas.

Do I place value on people? If you don't value and respect a person, you won't value his or her ideas. If you value people, you want to spend time with them, listen to them, want to help them, are influenced by them, and respect them.

Do I value the interactive process? A wonderful synergy often occurs as the result of shared thinking with those who bring informed opinions on a subject. It can take you places you've never been.

Write your answers to the three questions in today's reading to assess how much you truly want input from others.

DAY

75

Always be on the lookout for ideas. Be completely indiscriminate as to the source. Get ideas from customers, children, competitors, other industries, or cab drivers. It doesn't matter who thought of an idea.
JEFFREY J. FOX

A person who values cooperation and shared thinking desires to complete the ideas of others, not compete with them. If someone asks you to share ideas, focus on helping the team, not getting ahead personally—*move from competition to cooperation.* And if you are the one who brings people together to share their thoughts, praise the idea more than the source of the idea. If the best idea always wins (rather than the person who offered it), all will share their thoughts with greater enthusiasm.

When I spend time with someone to share ideas, I have an agenda. I know what I want to accomplish. The more I respect the wisdom of the person, the more I listen. For example, when I meet with someone I'm mentoring, I let the person ask the questions, but I expect to do most of the talking. When I meet with someone who mentors me, I mostly keep my mouth shut. In other relationships, the give and take is more even. But no matter with whom I meet, I have a reason for getting together and an expectation for what I'll give to it and get from it.

Examine every appointment or meeting you have listed for the coming week. Write down an objective for each. Interact with that objective in mind. Afterward, jot down any ideas that may have come as a result.

DAY

76

The lightning spark of thought generated in the solitary mind awakens its likeness in another mind.

THOMAS CARLYLE

The greatest secret to winning shared thinking is to *get the right people around the table.* As you prepare to ask people to participate in shared thinking, use the following criteria for the selection process. Choose people who . . .

- First and foremost desire the success of the ideas.
- Can add value to another's thoughts.
- Can emotionally handle the conversation.
- Appreciate others' strengths.
- Understand their place of value at the table.
- Place what is best for the team before themselves.
- Can bring out the best thinking in the people around them.
- Possess maturity, experience, and success in the issue.
- Will take ownership and responsibility for decisions.

Too often we choose our brainstorming partners based on feelings of friendship or circumstances or convenience. But that doesn't help us to discover and create the ideas of the highest order. Who we invite to the table makes all the difference.

Write a list of people you usually bring to the table to help you think. Or if you've not engaged in shared thinking before, make a list of people you would like to include. Now rate each person against the nine characteristics in my list. Give a point for each yes. This will help you see which people will be assets in shared thinking.

DAY

77

The strength of the team is each individual member.
The strength of each member is the team.
PHIL JACKSON

Successful organizations practice shared thinking. If you lead an organization, department, or team, you can't afford to be without people who are good at shared thinking. As you recruit and hire, look for good thinkers who value others, have experience with the collaborative process, and are emotionally secure. Then *compensate good thinkers and collaborators well* and challenge them to use their thinking skills and share their ideas often. Nothing adds value like a lot of good thinkers putting their minds together.

No matter what you're trying to accomplish, you can do it better with shared thinking. That is why I spend much of my life teaching leadership. Good leadership helps to put together the right people at the right time for the right purpose so that everybody wins. I'm such a strong believer in shared thinking that I engage in that process even when writing a book. My friends and colleagues make me better than I am alone. The same thing can happen for you. All it takes is the right people and a willingness to participate in shared thinking.

What specific ways are you realizing that your organization, department, or team needs to add more shared thinking times? What can you do to help make that happen?

DAY

78

*It is not the style of clothes one wears, neither the
kind of automobile one drives, nor the amount of money
one has in the bank, that counts. These mean nothing.
It is simply service that measures success.*
GEORGE WASHINGTON CARVER

Now I want to acquaint you with a kind of thinking with the potential to change your life in another way. It might even redefine how you view success.

In the 1890s, brilliant young George Washington Carver developed expertise in plant pathology and mycology and became the first African American faculty member at Iowa State College. He was respected professionally and poised to be rewarded with finances, position, and fame. Yet all of these things he gave up to move to the Tuskegee Institute in Alabama, in the heart of the deep South where he would be regarded as a second-class citizen.

If Carver had focused his attention on patenting his findings or building a business on his discoveries, he could have become a very rich man. But that was never his goal. His ideas proved especially successful at helping poor, black farmers of the South and earned him national respect. He spent his whole life focused on unselfish thinking, trying to help others. Carver found more than success. By thinking beyond himself, he discovered significance.

On a scale of 1 to 10, with 1 being always looking out for number one and 10 being focused on helping others, how do you rate yourself as an unselfish thinker? Write down three examples of where you were unselfish in your thinking and the positive results it netted.

DAY

79

There is no more noble occupation in the world than to assist another human being—to help someone succeed.
ALAN LOY MCGINNIS

Unselfish thinking can often deliver a return greater than any other kind of thinking. Few things in life bring greater personal rewards than helping others. Charles H. Burr believed, "Getters generally don't get happiness; givers get it." One of the benefits is that *unselfish thinking brings personal fulfillment.* When you spend your day unselfishly serving others, at night you can lay down your head with no regrets and sleep soundly. Helping people brings great satisfaction.

Even if you have spent much of your life pursuing selfish gain, it's never too late to have a change of heart. Even the most miserable person, like Charles Dickens' Scrooge, can turn his life around and make a difference for others. That's what Alfred Nobel did. When his brother died, Nobel saw his own obituary in the newspaper instead of his brother's. That was startling, but what shook him up the most was the newspaper's statement that Alfred Nobel's company, which produced explosives, had killed "more people faster than ever before." After seeing this, Nobel vowed to promote peace and acknowledge contributions to humanity. That is how the Nobel Prizes came into being.

Are you committed to putting others first and to developing and maintaining unselfish motives? Write a declaration of commitment to helping others. Then sign and date it.

DAY

80

He has achieved success who has lived well, laughed often and loved much; . . . who has always looked for the best in others and given them the best he had, whose life was an inspiration, whose memory a benediction.
BESSIE ANDERSON STANLEY

Of all the qualities a person can pursue, unselfish thinking seems to make the biggest difference toward *adding value to others* and *cultivating other virtues*. When you get outside of yourself and make a contribution to others, you really begin to live. I think that's because the ability to give unselfishly goes against the grain of human nature. But if you can learn to think unselfishly and become a giver, it becomes easier to develop many other virtues: gratitude, love, respect, patience, discipline, etc.

Unselfish thinking also increases quality of life. The spirit of generosity created by unselfish thinking gives people an appreciation for life and an understanding of its higher values. Seeing those in need and giving to meet that need puts a lot of things into perspective. It increases the quality of life of the giver and the receiver. That's why I believe that there is no life as empty as the self-centered life; there is no life as centered as the self-empty life. If you want to improve your world, focus your attention on helping others.

What assets do you have that could be used to invest in another person? What skills do you possess that someone would benefit from learning? What life experiences can be used to help another person? What resources do you possess that ought to be shared? Write out your list.

DAY

81

Learn, earn, return—these are the three phases of life. The first third should be devoted to education, the second third to building a career and making a living, and the last third to giving back to others—returning something in gratitude. Each state seems to be a preparation for the next one.

JACK BALOUSEK

Unselfish thinking makes you part of something greater than yourself and creates a legacy. In the mid 1980s, Merck and Company, the global pharmaceutical corporation, developed a drug to cure river blindness, a disease that causes blindness in millions of people, particularly in developing countries where potential customers couldn't afford to buy it. Merck developed the drug anyway and announced that it would give the medicine free to anyone who needed it. As of 1998, the company had given more than 250 million tablets away. George W. Merck said, "We try never to forget that medicine is for the people. It is not for the profits. The profits follow, and if we have remembered that, they have never failed to appear."

The lesson to be learned? Simple. Instead of trying to be great, be part of something greater than yourself. If you are successful, it becomes possible for you to leave an inheritance *for* others. But if you desire to do more, to create a legacy, you need to leave that *in* others.

Set giving goals for yourself. What can you do to help others that will in no way benefit you (other than to give you internal satisfaction)? Set an amount of money to give away this year (anonymously, if possible). Decide on a number of hours a week or month to serve others. Find a cause that you can help to succeed.

DAY

82

*People with humility don't think less of themselves;
they just think of themselves less.*

KEN BLANCHARD
and NORMAN VINCENT PEALE

Most people recognize the value of unselfish thinking and agree that it's an ability they would like to develop. To begin cultivating the ability to think unselfishly, *put others first.* You need to stop thinking about your wants and begin focusing on others' needs. Paul the Apostle exhorted, "Do nothing out of selfish ambition or vain conceit, but in humility consider others better than yourselves. Each of you should look not only to your own interests, but also to the interests of others." Make a mental and emotional commitment to look out for the interests of others.

Then *expose yourself to situations where people have needs.* To make the transition, put yourself in a position where you can see people's needs and do something about it. Once you do, follow the advice of Tod Barnhart, "Act with impact—you've got to give to live!" The kind of giving you do isn't important at first. You can make donations to a food bank, volunteer professional services, serve at your church, or give to a charitable organization. The point is to learn how to give and to cultivate the habit of thinking like a giver.

During the coming week, tune your intuitive radar to look for needs in others. What needs do you perceive and feel prompted to help? Don't wait. Take action!

DAY

83

What seems to be generosity is often no more than disguised ambition, which overlooks a small interest in order to secure a great one.

FRANÇOIS DE LA ROCHEFOUCAULD

Once you have learned to give of yourself, the next step is to learn to *give quietly or anonymously*. It's almost always easier to give when you receive recognition for it than it is when no one is likely to know about it. The people who give in order to receive a lot of fanfare, however, have already received any reward they will get. There are spiritual, mental, and emotional benefits that come only to those who give anonymously. If you've never given when you cannot receive anything in return, try it.

The hardest thing is fighting our natural tendency to put ourselves first. That's why it's important to *continually examine your motives* to make sure you're not sliding backwards into selfishness. Follow the modeling of Benjamin Franklin. Every day, he asked himself two questions. When he got up in the morning, he would ask, "What good am I going to do today?" And before he went to bed, he would ask, "What good have I done today?" If you can answer those questions with selflessness and integrity, you can keep yourself on track.

In the morning, ask yourself, "What good am I going to do today?" And before your go to bed, ask, "What good have I done today?" Be honest with yourself in your answers. Make this a habit every day and note how it changes your life.

DAY

84

*If you will help others achieve what they want,
they will help you achieve what you want.*
ZIG ZIGLER

The highest level of unselfish thinking comes when you give of yourself to another person for their personal development or well-being. If you want to become the kind of person who invests in people, consider others and their journey so that you can collaborate with them. Each relationship is like a partnership created for mutual benefit. As you go into any relationship, think about how you can invest in the other person so it becomes a win-win situation. Here is how relationships most often play out:

I win, you lose—I win only once.

You win, I lose—You win only once.

We both win—We win many times.

We both lose—Goodbye, partnership!

The best relationships are win-win. Why don't more people go into relationships with that attitude? I'll tell you why: Most people want to make sure that they win first. Unselfish thinkers, on the other hand, go into a relationship and make sure that the other person wins first. And that makes all the difference.

Think about a current or imminent professional goal that you would like to make a win-win. What must you do for your part to create that? And what effort will you make to guarantee that the other person wins first?

DAY

85

We kept asking ourselves very simple questions.
What is our business? Who is our customer? And what
does the customer consider value? If you're the Girl Scouts,
IBM, or AT&T, you have to manage for a mission.

FRANCES HESSELBEIN

How do you figure out the bottom line for your organization, business, department, team, or group? In many businesses, the bottom line is literally the bottom line. Profit determines whether you are succeeding. But dollars should not always be the primary measure of success. How would you measure the success of your family or the bottom line of a volunteer organization?

Frances Hesselbein had to ask herself exactly that question in 1976, when she became the national executive director of the Girl Scouts of America. At the time, the organization lacked direction, teenage girls were losing interest in scouting, and it was becoming increasingly difficult to recruit adult volunteers. Hesselbein's focus on mission enabled her to identify the Girl Scouts' bottom line: "We really are here for one reason: to help a girl reach her highest potential." That enabled her to create a strategy to try to achieve it. In 1990, Hesselbein left the Girl Scouts after making it a first-class organization, having established a bottom line not measured in dollars, but in changed lives.

On a scale of 1 to 10, with 1 being goal-less thinking and 10 being bottom-line thinking, how do you rate yourself as a bottom-line thinker? Write down three examples of where your thinking was focused on the bottom line and the positive results it netted.

DAY

86

*There ain't no rules around here.
We're trying to accomplish something.*
THOMAS EDISON

If you're accustomed to thinking of the bottom line only as it relates to financial matters, you may be missing some things crucial to you and your organization. Instead, think of the bottom line as the end, the take away, the desired result. Every activity has its own unique bottom line. If you have a job, are a parent, have a spouse, or serve in your church, you have bottom lines for each activity and relationship.

As you explore the concept of bottom-line thinking, recognize that it *provides great clarity*. Bottom-line thinking makes it possible for you to measure outcomes more quickly and easily. It gives you a benchmark by which to measure activity. It can be used as a focused way of ensuring that all your little activities are purposeful and line up to achieve a larger goal. It *helps you assess every situation*. When you know your bottom line, it becomes much easier to know how you're doing in any given area. There's no better measurement tool than the bottom line.

What is your personal bottom line? Why are you doing what you're doing in your career? What are you trying to accomplish in your family life? Can you describe what purpose you believe you've been put on this earth to accomplish?

DAY

87

A small body of determined spirits fired by an unquenchable faith in their mission can alter the course of history.

MAHATMA GANDHI

When the Girl Scouts were struggling in the 1970s, outside organizations tried to convince its members to become women's rights activists or door-to-door canvassers. But under Hesselbein, it became easy to say no. The people in the organization knew their bottom line and wanted to pursue their goals with focus and fervency. Bottom-line thinking *helps you make the best decisions.*

Bottom-line thinking also *generates high morale.* When you know the bottom line and go after it, you greatly increase your odds of winning. And nothing generates high morale like winning. Sports teams that win the championship, or company divisions that achieve their goals, or volunteers who achieve their mission get excited. Hitting the target feels exhilarating. And you can hit it only if you know what it is.

If you want to be successful tomorrow, you need to think bottom line today. Bottom-line thinking *ensures your future.* Look at any successful, lasting company, and you'll find leaders who know their bottom line. They make their decisions, allocate their resources, hire their people, and structure their organization to achieve that bottom line.

Give some thought to your career, family, recreation, service, and life purpose. Work to write succinctly your bottom line for each. Then use these statements as your guiding principles for decision-making.

DAY

88

*Set yourself earnestly to see what you were made to do,
and then set yourself earnestly to do it.*
PHILLIPS BROOKS

It isn't hard to see the value of the bottom line. Most people would agree that bottom-line thinking has a high return. But learning how to be a bottom-line thinker can be challenging. The process begins with *identifying the real bottom line*—knowing what you're going after. It can be as lofty as the big-picture vision, mission, or purpose of an organization. Or it can be as focused as what you want to accomplish on a particular project. What's important is that you be as specific as possible. If your goal is for something as vague as "success," you will have a painfully difficult time trying to harness bottom-line thinking to achieve it.

One of the things you can do to improve your bottom-line thinking is to set aside your personal "wants." Instead, try to get to the results you're *really* looking for, the true essence of the goal. You can also set aside any emotions that may cloud your judgment, and you can remove any politics that may influence your perception. What are you really trying to achieve? When you strip away all the things that don't really matter, what are you compelled to achieve? What must occur? What is acceptable? That is the real bottom line.

Chose a major area of your life or career to examine. Then set aside a block of time to determine the bottom line for this area and write it here. What are you really trying to achieve?

DAY

89

Great leaders have a heart for people.
They take time for people. They view people as
the bottom line, not as a tool to get to the bottom line.

PAT WILLIAMS

Have you ever been in a conversation with someone whose intentions seem other than stated? Sometimes the situation reflects intentional deception. But it can also occur when the person doesn't know his own bottom line.

The same thing happens in companies. Sometimes, for example, an idealistically stated mission and the real bottom line don't jibe. Purpose and profits compete. You must *make the bottom line the point.* Earlier, I quoted George W. Merck, who stated, "We try never to forget that medicine is for the people. It is not for the profits. The profits follow, and if we have remembered that, they have never failed to appear." He probably made that statement to remind those in his organization that profits *serve* purpose—they don't compete with it.

If making a profit were the only real bottom line, and helping people merely provided the means for achieving it, the company would suffer. Its attention would be divided, and it would neither help people as well as it could nor make as much profit as it desired.

Continuing with yesterday's thought, now that you have made the bottom line your point of emphasis, not a substitute for another unstated goal or just a step toward it, develop a strategy for accomplishing the bottom line.

DAY

90

What an immense power over the life is the power of possessing distinct aims. The voice, the dress, the look, the very motions of a person, define and alter when he or she begins to live for a reason.
ELIZABETH STUART PHELPS

Bottom-line thinking achieves results. Therefore, it naturally follows that *any plans that flow out of such thinking must tie directly to the bottom line*—and there can be only one main one, not two or three. In organizations, that often means identifying the core elements or functions that must operate properly to achieve the bottom line. This is the leader's responsibility. The important thing is that when the bottom line of each activity is achieved, then THE bottom line is achieved. If the sum of the smaller goals doesn't add up to the real bottom line, either your strategy is flawed or you've not identified your real bottom line.

Once you have your strategy in place, *make sure your people line up with your strategy.* Ideally, all team members should know the big goal, as well as their individual role in achieving it.

Regardless of your bottom line, you can improve it with good thinking. And bottom-line thinking has a great return because it helps to turn your ideas into results and to reap the full potential of your thinking.

You are the leader of your own life. Think about what your bottom line is and what you want your legacy to be. Write it down, and strive to focus your thinking toward creating it.

Look for the next book in the JumpStart series

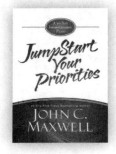

The way you prioritize and spend your time each day greatly impacts your ability to succeed. With this 90-day improvement plan by #1 *New York Times* bestselling author John C. Maxwell, you will learn to master the moment and reach your goals by setting the right priorities and executing on them. Whether you are just starting out in your career or looking to expand on your achievements, this resource will help you focus and achieve. Combining engaging lessons, thought-provoking questions, inspiring quotes, and journaling space to track your progress, Maxwell delivers daily inspiration and practical advice to help you maximize the potential of the most important day of your life—today.

Coming in summer 2016 from Center Street
wherever books are sold.

CENTER
STREET

NEW YORK · BOSTON · NASHVILLE

Introducing the JumpStart Series Community on Facebook

Find other fans of the JumpStart series and maximize your personal and professional growth.

- Interact with other like-minded leaders.
- Receive and share inspiring quotes with your friends.
- Engage with thought-provoking questions and answers.
- Get the latest news about upcoming books in the JumpStart series and receive exclusive information.
- Experience a daily community where you can get ideas on how to apply what you learn.

Visit www.facebook.com/TheJumpStartSeries
and Like the page to get started.